Explore The Ruins with Mario & Luigi

OrangeBooks Publication

1st Floor, Rajhans Arcade, Mall Road, Kohka, Bhilai, Chhattisgarh 490020

Website: **www.orangebooks.in**

First Edition, 2024

ISBN: 978-93-6554-088-8

GEM SEARCHERS

Vir Krishn Khanna

AUTHOR AND ILLUSTRATOR

OrangeBooks Publication

www.orangebooks.in

Dedication

To my mamu; for introducing me to videogames.

And to my Bua; for introducing me to the Nintendo world.

About the Author

Vir Krishn Khanna is passionate about Books and his Nintendo Switch. This book is inspired by Vir's love for wordplay and the world of Mario Super Bros. He sometimes wishes he could Pipe into the Mario world himself, and leave Delhi behind. Vir has been writing stories and making his own books since he was 5; Vir's passion for drawing helps him create stories that he hopes will build a connection with others.

About the Book

Mario has been searching for the Super Star for ages. He has finally deduced that he needs all the Gems, starting with the gem of Love. However, other people want it too.

Will Mario succeed or will he be crushed by Rainbow Bowser?

The Star Prophecy

If thou want the Super Star
You must take a journey, very far

First for courage, shining green
Row through waters, a rough scene

Next for love, take a friend
Work together, for a blue gem

Third, Tenacity, blazing red
Persevere, do not shed

Next in yellow, fun and fame
Dance through a musical game

Finally, passion, purple, very fine
Make it through the challenges in time

If you get all 5 gemstones
Then the bell will toll
Bringing afoot the Super Star
Healing all your woes and scars

Prologue

Luigi's Point of View

When I reached Mario's room, he was still snoring.

I sighed. I had no choice. I had to bring out my alarming alarm clock- the BOOscreamer.

As it rang, Mario shot out of bed and glared at me, still in his pajamas.

"HOW MANY TIMES HAVE I TOLD YOU NOT TO USE THE BOOSCREAMER!" He screeched!

I shook my head in exasperation. "Did you forget *again?* "I asked him. "We're going to the Whomps Domino Ruins today".

Contents

The Mario Viewpoint

1. The First Team 1
2. Ally Ambition 4
3. Instantaneous Items 6
4. Problematic Pinball 8
5. Starscape Sightseeing 10
6. Virtuous Victory 12

Chapter — 1

The First Team

When Luigi and I reached the ruins, Koopa Troopa and Kamek were waiting for us. With a few flicks of his wand, Kamek made different scrolls appear, explaining the rules of the game. With a flick of his wrist, he and Koopa Troopa disappeared.

Then the other team floated down in bubbles, popping to reveal a blank-eyed Goomba, and some sort of pupil-less chipmunk with wings. In the air,

Bowser and Bowser Jr. were in flycarts, ordering them around.

During turn rolling, we got a 9 and the other team got a 4. Bowser breathed fire angrily, but I dodged it. Since we could move seven spaces, I ran for an Item Space, while Luigi stomped the other team. However, their 5 movable spaces let them stomp Luigi. The minigame was Just For Kicks, and it looked odd since it was two vs two. We won, since Bowser and Bowser Jr. didn't seem to work together very well.

Oh, if you're new- I'll tell you something. The Super Star gives you invincibility and turns you into a rainbow. See, my friend Peach apparently loves rainbows. And Bowser is *head over heels (talons?)* in love with Peach. He thinks that stealing the Super Star and transforming into a rainbow version of himself will make Peach fall in love with him. Ha!

The way to get the Super Star is to get all the Gems of Good Traits-Spirit, Tenacity, Love, Courage, and Passion. The way to get the Gemstones is to complete all the challenges, stages, boards, and branches of The Party Challenge. And only the "Chosen One" can do it.

Recently, the Tattletale Toad(the local fortune teller)prophesied that me and my gang were the Chosen Ones. So we decided to take on the Party Challenge. Me and Luigi called getting the Gem of Love.

So here we are. In a shadowy, scary ruin filled with giganto things that might fall on us. Not what I would call an ideal situation.

Chapter — 2
Ally Ambition

Since Round 1 was done, Allies started floating down. If you run through one, they follow you around and give you extra rolls of the dice.

I don't think Bowser is too bright, since he ordered his minions to move away from the star.

But they also got a lot of allies by moving into them. Soon DK, Shy Guy, Fire Bro, Boomerang Bro, and Diddy Kong were following them.

Luigi and I also got a few allies; We used ally phones, and Peach, Daisy, Rosalina, Yoshi, Toad, and Toadette came to us.

But having lots of allies on the platform meant that there was very little space to move in the game without having to bring out a quick cursor and wasting time on selecting allies. It was also hard to chose which dice blocks to use since one is dependent on their dice.

Soon, ally mini-games popped up. Since we had dueling gloves, we used them in minigames to steal allies. Train for Pain, Half the Battle, Just for Kicks, and Bumper Brawl were very chaotic. Everybody was crashing into each other and were aching all over by the end. Bowser even ordered his minions to massage him (WHAT?!)

"I wish the allies would just reset," grumbled Luigi as he shoved Boo out of the way and got throttled by Sledge Bro

Chapter – 3

Instantaneous Items

Since item spaces are very useful, many people landed on them on their way to the star.

But It was mostly fly guy tickets. The tickets were used to summon fly guys and steal items. People were using Fly Guys to steal Fly Guy tickets and there was a lot of confusion. The mere sight of a Fly Guy dragging another Fly Guy along was enough to make you gag with laughter.

It is insane how mean you can be with fly guys. Once the other team had a double star card, and we used a fly guy to steal it.

Another way to get items is to buy them from a shop. Shops are identifiable by their cloudy sphere icon. They offer *amazing* deals- I mean, a *Golden Mushroom* for just 5 coins. That's like, *too* cheap. In the Kingdom of Mushrooms, they cost like, *50 coins* indirectly for Good Luck Tickets (*that's* how rarely a Coin Vendor will spit them out.)

Chapter – 4
Problematic Pinball

After a star snatch, the star flew up to the pinball rails. Every normal rail was a Pinball activator; (*If you landed in a pin place, the pinball sent you back and took away 5 of your coins.*) For some reason, people always seemed to do poorly in minigames after they got hit, probably because getting hit gave them a headache.

I was getting fed up. Every time we tried to get close to the star, we got sent back to the beginning. I told Luigi to stay near the star, but out of the Pinball range.

There is absolutely NO way to dodge a pinball (well, unless you want to to run back to the start)

Since Pinnies (that's what I call them) are so destructive, Bowser tried to corrupt the system so that it only worked on Luigi and I, and ended up being given Bad Luck for the game.

You can also use Pinnies as modes of getting to- *(pinball hits Mario in the head-)*" YOWCH!MAMMA MIA!*(panting)* the-star or even to attack your enemies. For example, you could activate a Pinnie and then run out of the way, getting your opponent hit in the head.

Chapter – 5

Starscape Sightseeing

Bowser looked at me. He ordered Goomba to open up an odd jar. A Coinado came out and stole my coins. Then, the chipmunk sent a fly guy at Luigi, taking his skeleton key. Goomba took a Lakitu Lumber to the star and bought it, then Boo went to the chests and bought another star from their depths with the key, putting them in the lead!

Me and Luigi also bought stars. However, the final 2 turns were near. The other team was still ahead!

"What happens if we lose"? Luigi asked. "We get kept in the waiting room forever," I told him. "Our avatars never get chosen."

Luigi was trembling. I was worried too, and Luigi looked like he was about to cry. I felt the same, but what could we do? It was the last 2 turns. We were about to lose! Mamma Mia!

However, Bowser's Bad Luck M was about to bring us victory

Chapter – 6
Virtuous Victory

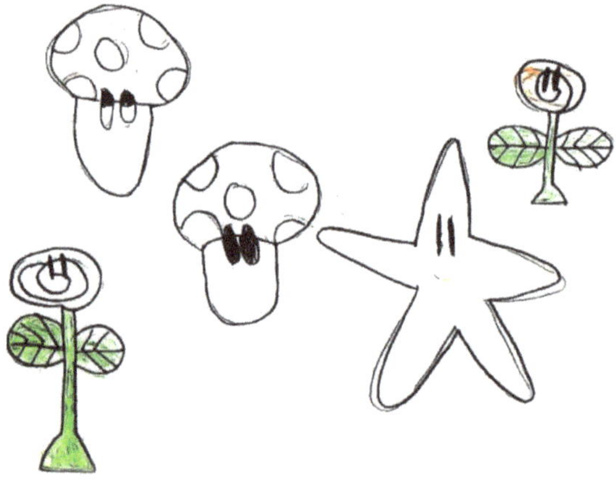

Toad blew a whistle- it was the homestretch bonus

We were given 20 coins and a Star Pipe. We warped to the stars, and bought them

Toad blew the End Game whistle. It was all down to the bonus stars.

First, a star with "Buddy Bonus" etched neatly on it was given to me and Luigi. Toad explained that we got them for having Peach and Daisy as allies.

Then, a star with "Losing Bonus" was given to Goomba. But it wasn't enough to bring them into the lead!

Soon, the other team was getting smashed by Whomps and then inserted into bubbles to be floated away.

Meanwhile, we had a huge party! The Gem of Love was presented to us, along with a map on how to get to the next level. At the party, there were power flowers, mushrooms, and coins. The best part was, when we got to meet the King Whomp Mashman live!

"I'm excited for level 2," Luigi grinned. I was also excited, the game had been lots of fun. Bring it on!

Epilogue

The Bowser Point of View

As soon as we got back to the castle, I summoned the Goomba and Chipmunk.

"You failed me". I growled dangerously.

"It wasn't our fault sir, you were control- (cut off in the middle).

I crushed the Goomba with one step, and ripped the Chipmunk's wings off. As it fainted in agony, I turned to my Koopa force. "Bring me the next level minions" I said."

I need my Super Star... (trails off).

www.ingramcontent.com/pod-product-compliance
Ingram Content Group UK Ltd.
Pitfield, Milton Keynes, MK11 3LW, UK
UKHW050029160325
456163UK00020B/79

9 789365 540888